THE SUPPRESSION OF THE RELIGIOUS HOUSES IN BRISTOL

Joseph Bettey

By the later Middle Ages the wealth and piety of the merchant community in Bristol had ensured that the busy port was dominated and surrounded by churches, religious houses, chantries, chapels, hospitals and other ecclesiastical institutions. Eighteen parish churches were crowded in and around the walls of the town, while there were religious houses on all sides.[1]

The oldest religious house was the Benedictine priory of St James, which had been founded in the twelfth century as a cell or subsidiary house of the wealthy monastery at Tewkesbury. Although this was a small priory with only three or four monks, it occupied an important site by the Horsefair, and controlled the land on which St James Fair was held in July each year, playing a leading part in the economic life of the town. Since 1374 the nave of the priory church had been used as a parish church and the priory was also the patron of several other parish churches in Bristol.

The importance of Bristol as a port and urban centre is illustrated by the fact that the four major orders of friars all had houses in the town. The Black Friars or Dominicans were established in Broadmead, the Grey Friars or Franciscans in Lewins Mead, the friary of the Augustinian or Austin Friars was near Temple Gate, and the White Friars or Carmelites were situated near the site of the present Colston Hall.[2] The Friars were

---

1. The monastic houses, parish churches and other religious institutions of Bristol are listed and described in J.F. Nichols and John Taylor, *Bristol Past and Present*, II, 1881, and also in *Victoria County History of Gloucestershire*, II, 1907, 74–119.
2. D. Knowles and R.N. Hadcock, *Medieval Religious Houses in England and Wales*, 1953, 183, 189, 196, 200, 227.

dedicated to poverty and to preaching the gospel, and their friaries remained poor and sparsely furnished, with unremarkable buildings, but each had a large church designed for preaching, and as will be shown later, preaching in the friary churches played an important part in preparing the way for the Reformation in Bristol.

By far the wealthiest and most splendid of the religious houses in Bristol was that of the Augustinian canons, whose church was later to become the cathedral. This had also been founded in the twelfth century, and by the late Middle Ages was a well-endowed establishment with lands and estates in Bristol as well as in Somerset and Gloucestershire, bringing it a large income and supporting an abbot and some twenty canons.[3] At the foot of St Michael's Hill there was a small house of Augustinian canonesses which had also been founded in the twelfth century, although like so many of the religious houses for women, it remained small and poorly-endowed.

In addition, there were numerous chapels, chantries, almshouses and hospitals throughout the town, including the Hospital of St Mark, known as the Gaunts Hospital, with its fine church and domestic buildings on College Green. It is not possible to include in this short pamphlet an account of the fortunes of all the various hospitals and chapelries during the upheavals of the Reformation period, but details will be given concerning the suppression of St Mark's, since the master and chaplains of this important charitable foundation for the poor, sick and aged followed the Rule of St Benedict.[4]

Throughout the Middle Ages Bristol was situated at the extreme edge of the large diocese of Worcester, which extended down the Severn and included much of Worcestershire and Gloucestershire. The suburbs of Redcliffe, Temple, St Thomas and Bedminster were in the diocese of Bath and Wells. The town was thus remote from episcopal supervision, and the monastic houses, especially St Augustine's, were of great importance in the religious and social life of the community. For example, it was at St Augustine's that important visitors to Bristol were accommodated. Henry VII and

---

3. G. Beachcroft and A. Sabin, eds., 'Two Compotus Rolls of St Augustine's Abbey, Bristol', *Bristol Record Society*, IX, 1938.
4. C.D. Ross, ed., 'Cartulary of St Mark's Hospital, Bristol', *Bristol Record Society*, XXI, 1959.

his queen stayed there for three days in 1486, Archbishop Cranmer was lodged there during his visitation of Bristol in 1534 and in 1535 Henry VIII and Anne Boleyn proposed to stay there and were only deterred at the last moment by an outbreak of the plague in Bristol.[5] The Abbot of St Augustine's was one of the most powerful and influential persons in Bristol, the abbey owned many properties in the town and neighbourhood and also controlled the patronage of many parish churches. From the surviving late-medieval account rolls of the abbey it is possible to obtain a good impression of the wealth of the institution and of the way in which its affairs were managed. Its urban property included houses, shops, inns, a water-mill and a rope-walk in Bristol, whilst it also possessed large estates in Gloucestershire, Somerset, Dorset and South Wales. Most of these properties were let to tenants and the rents went to maintain the abbot and canons. By the end of the fifteenth century the net annual income was some £700. Besides the support of the religious, the expenditure included the maintenance of the fine buildings, the costs of the services, together with the sumptuous vestments, lights and other expensive items, the charges of a school for the choir boys, the support of students at Oxford, hospitality and the distribution of alms to the poor and needy. The accounts show that the income was carefully husbanded and that there was no undue waste or lavish expenditure, but nonetheless an increasing number of the citizens of Bristol may have questioned whether the prayers of the canons could justify such a large outlay on their support, and this may partly explain why, at the end, no voices were raised in Bristol to support the canons.[6]

Relations between the religious houses and the townsmen were not always harmonious in the decades before the Reformation. A bitter dispute between the Abbot of St Augustine's and the town officials over their respective rights and jurisdiction lasted from 1491 to 1496 and required the intervention of the Archbishop of Canterbury and the Lord Chief Justice before it was settled. A further dispute in 1515 led to violent clashes between the two sides, while in the 1520s during a controversy over taxes the Mayor imprisoned some of the abbey servants, and the Abbot and canons

5. J.H. Bettey, *Bristol Observed*, 1986, 21–33.
6. G. Beachcroft and A. Sabin, *op. cit.*

Bristol Cathedral Chapter House

The Chapter House of c. 1170 together with its entrance from the cloister is the finest piece of Romanesque architecture in Bristol, and is an impressive reminder of the wealth and splendour of the Augustinian abbey
(J. Britton, *History and Antiquities of Bristol Cathedral, 1836*)

stormed the prison in an unsuccessful attempt to release them. Again the matter had to be settled by arbitration.[7]

But such quarrels were exceptional, in general the townsmen of Bristol accepted that the religious houses, like the parish churches, were part of the natural order. Even as late as 1530, few would have been so rash as to predict that within ten years there would be no more monks or nuns throughout the whole of England, that the friaries would have been totally abolished and that all the vast monastic wealth, widespread estates. splendid buildings and all their treasures would have passed into the hands of the Crown. The rest of this pamphlet will describe how this was accomplished and the results which it had in Bristol.

The suppression of the monasteries, nunneries and friaries throughout England and Wales during the period 1536–40 took place against the background of dramatic changes in the Church in England, notably the renunciation of the power of the Pope and the elevation of the King to the title of Supreme Head of the Church in 1534. In Bristol these changes were heralded and accompanied by fierce controversy and violent debate conducted by preachers in some of the numerous churches. In this 'battle of the pulpits' the friars played a leading part and one of the central issues was the usefulness of the religious houses.[8] There were already numerous critics of the Church in Bristol, although it is impossible to gain any clear idea of the views of the majority, but there are indications that some at least were ready to welcome reform in the Church, including suppression of the religious houses.

In 1533 Hugh Latimer, who was already well known as a preacher and leading supporter of reform, was invited by the mayor of Bristol to deliver three Lenten sermons in the town. The sermons were preached from the pulpits of St Nicholas, St Thomas and the Black Friars. Latimer's eloquent advocacy of reform provoked equally spirited replies from conservatives among the clergy, including a stout defence of the established order from

---

7. Gloucester Public Library, Hockaday Abstracts 428; *Victoria County History of Gloucestershire*, II, 1907, 78; see also Elizabeth Ralph, ed., 'The Great White Book of Bristol', *Bristol Record Society*, XXXII, 1979, 17–67.
8. G.R. Elton, *Policy and Police*, 1972, 112–20; K.G. Powell, 'The Beginnings of Protestantism in Gloucestershire', *Bristol & Gloucestershire Archaeological Society Transactions*, 90, 1971, 141–57.

John Hilsey, prior of the Dominicans, and from Robert Cicestre, prior of St James. The violent disputes which were occasioned by the rival orators reached the ears of the King's chief minister, Thomas Cromwell, who appointed a commission to enquire into the matter headed by William Burton, the abbot of St Augustine's abbey. The commission condemned both parties for the 'infamy, discord, strife and debate' they had created. The future was to lie with the reformers, however, for in 1535 Hugh Latimer was appointed Bishop of Worcester and thus became the ecclesiastical overlord of Bristol. Controversy and debate over religious reform continued intermittently in Bristol through 1535, 1536 and 1537, as rival preachers proclaimed their views or refuted those of their opponents. Again the friars with their tradition of lively preaching were in the forefront and, for example, in 1537 Robert Sanderson the prior of the Franciscans in Lewins Mead preached a Lenten sermon which stressed the old values, while William Oliver, who had succeeded Hilsey as prior of the Dominicans in Broadmead, championed the reforming cause and denounced the whole concept of monasteries and friaries, declaring that 'a whole shipload laden with friars' girdles and a dung-cart full of monks' cowls would avail nothing without faith'.[9]

It was against this background of religious controversy and popular argument that the suppression of the religious houses in Bristol was to take place. The first step came in 1534 with the Act of Supremacy to which all monks and friars were ordered to signify their assent. Whatever misgivings they may have felt about the Act, the abbot of St Augustine's and eighteen canons acknowledged the royal supremacy over the Church on 9 September 1534; likewise the prior of St James and four monks, while two days later the master of St Mark's Hospital and four brethren signed their agreement. The friars with their historical relationship with the Papacy were more reluctant, and in 1534 John Hilsey, who had been prior of the Bristol Dominicans, was appointed as Provincial or head of the Dominican order in England and was charged by the King with the task of securing the assent of all the English friaries to the royal supremacy. Many friars fled abroad rather than subscribe their assent, but eventually Hilsey obtained the submission of all those who remained.[10]

9. *Ibid.*
10. *Letters and Papers of Henry VIII*, VII, 1216, *V.C.H. Gloucestershire*, II, 1907, 10.

No doubt the religious who accepted the royal supremacy over the Church and at the same time acquiesced in the repudiation of Katherine of Aragon and the royal marriage to Anne Boleyn, saw no alternative in the face of royal power and the pressure that was put upon them. Many may have hoped that time would change the situation, but the fact that they had solemnly accepted the royal supremacy left them with little defence during all the upheavals which were so soon to follow.

During 1535 the national attack upon the religious houses was put in motion under the administrative genius of Thomas Cromwell, and the effects of his policy were soon to be felt in Bristol. Cromwell's first move was to order a detailed enquiry into the wealth of the religious houses and other ecclesiastical institutions, the *Valor Ecclesiasticus* which revealed for the first time and in detail the enormous wealth of the Church. The collection of so much information was a prodigious task and it is a tribute to Cromwell's energy and efficiency that most of the returns were complete by the autumn of 1535, showing for the religious houses all sources of revenue, the gross annual income and all payments which each house was obliged to make under the terms of its foundation or subsequent bequests. With such a massive undertaking, conducted over such a short period, there are inevitably some errors and omissions, and St Augustine's abbey in Bristol was either overlooked or the returns were lost. But the wealth of St Augustine's can be determined from other sources, and the wealth of the Bristol houses in 1535 can therefore be summarised as follows:

Valor Ecclesiasticus

Religious House	Order	No. of Religious	Net Annual Income in 1535
St James Priory	Benedictine	5	£55 7s 4d
St Augustine's Abbey	Augustinian	19	£670 0s 0d
St Mary Magdalen	Augustinian Canonesses	2	£21 0s 0d
St Mark's Hosp.	Benedictine	5	£102 0s 0d

The surviving late-medieval records of St Augustine's abbey give a very clear picture of its wealth, the extent of its lands and of the way in which the monastic economy was managed. As well as numerous properties in Bristol, the abbey possessed lands at eleven places in Gloucestershire, six in Somerset, one in Dorset and two in Wales. It also received the great tithes of more than twenty appropriated parish churches. Most of the lands were let to tenants and were managed for the abbey by bailiffs, but a supply of foodstuffs, timber and firewood came up the Avon to the abbey from its manors of Abbots Leigh and Portbury.

The expenditure included maintenance of the buildings, food, drink and clothing for the canons, an allowance for the separate establishment of the abbot, servants' wages and the costs of hospitality and charity.[11]

Before the work of the commissioners sent by Cromwell to compile the *Valor Ecclesiasticus* was complete, another visitation of the monasteries had begun. This second group of commissioners was charged by Cromwell with the task of enquiring into the state of the religious houses, and if possible they were to produce evidence of laxity, scandal, neglect of religious vows and failure to live up to monastic ideals. Such evidence could then be used by Cromwell to justify at least a partial suppression. The commissioner who visited Bristol in August 1535 was Richard Layton, a young, energetic and ambitious priest, who was keen to rise in Cromwell's service. The numerous letters and reports which he sent to Cromwell show a total contempt for the monasteries, scorn for many contemporary religious practices, especially for the veneration of relics, and a facility for finding or inventing gossip and salacious stories about the moral failings of the monks and nuns.[12] He came to Bristol from visiting the religious houses at Bath, Maiden Bradley, Bruton and the great Benedictine abbey at Glastonbury. From Bristol he wrote to Cromwell on 24 August 1535 describing with obvious relish the irregularities he claimed to have found at Maiden Bradley and sending a collection of relics which he had confiscated from the religious houses. At Bruton and Glastonbury, however, he had been unable to find anything wrong and regretfully reported to Cromwell that the monks were kept under such strict discipline that they could not misbehave, adding

11. A. Sabin, ed., 'Some Manorial Accounts of St Augustine's, Bristol', *Bristol Record Society*, 22, 1960.
12. For a full account of the commissioners' findings in the Bristol region see J.H. Bettey, *Suppression of the Monasteries in the West Country*, 1989, 43–56.

West Front of the Benedictine Priory of St James

Because it was used as a parish church, this fine nave survived the dissolution, although the chancel and domestic buildings were rapidly destroyed

with obvious disappointment, 'but fain they would if they might, as they confess, and so the fault is not in them'.[13]

Likewise at Bristol, Layton could apparently find nothing wrong. This is a tribute to the religious life in the Bristol houses, for if he could have found anything amiss Layton would assuredly have reported on it. In fact we are dependent upon a quite different source for the only piece of gossip which survives about the religious in Bristol during the 1530s. This comes from the evidence presented in a case before the Bishop's Court at Worcester in 1540 after the monasteries had been suppressed and concerns John Rastle or Rastall who had been a canon at St Augustine's. Rastle had been nominated to be a chantry priest at Winterbourne in Gloucestershire, but various objections were made against him before the Bishop. Previously he had been sent by St Augustine's as a student to Oxford where he may have acquired bad habits, for it was alleged that when he returned to Bristol he had become an obsessive card-player, dicer and gambler. Nicholas Corbett, who had been a fellow canon at St Augustine's, told the court that Rastle was a well-known gambler and that Rastle had 'got at dice and cards of divers men in his chamber in the late monastery, £10, £5 and 5 marks (£3 6s 8d), especially in the year before the dissolution of the said Monastery'. Another witness, John Wyggen of Bristol stated that he had 'known one to lose £10 to the said Rastle, and afterwards to sell the coate off his back, and lost the price thereof, playing at cards with the said Rastle'. Notwithstanding this evidence, Rastle was instituted to the chantry by the bishop.[14] This is the only evidence which has come to light about any irregularity or scandal in the Bristol religious houses and it either escaped the notice of Layton, or probably did not occur until after his visitation in 1535.

One result of Layton's visit to St Augustine's was that on his departure he ordered the Abbot, that neither he nor any of his canons should go outside the precinct of the abbey, that the monastic Rule should be strictly observed, and that no lay persons, especially women, should be allowed inside the abbey. Immediately the Abbot wrote a servile letter to Cromwell protesting at the restrictions and asking for them to be relaxed.

---

13. T. Wright, ed., 'Letters relating the Suppression of the Monasteries', *Camden Society*, 26, 1843, 7–10, 58–9.
14. Gloucester Public Library, Hockaday Abstracts, Winterbourne file.

Right honourable Mr Secretary, Principal Visitor under the King's most royal majesty, supreme head of the church of England next under God in earth. So it is that the reverend and discreet man Master Doctor Layton by his great authority lately visited us at the King's monastery of St Austins where he left at his gentle departing with me and my brethren certain injunctions somewhat hard and strait to be observed and kept. Whereof I most heartily desire your good mastership to grant me and to my officer chamberlain licence and liberty to go and to ride to see good order, custom, and manner to be kept within the lordships of the said monastery at times convenient for the profits of the same. Secondly I heartily pray you to give me licence and liberty to walk to my manor places nigh to Bristol for the comfortable health of my body and for the saving of expenses. Thirdly I beseech you that I may walk within the circuit of the monastery, that is to say within the Green and Canons Marsh next adjacent to the precincts of the said monastery. Furthermore both I and my brethren instantly prayeth, desireth, and beseecheth your good mastership to grant to me power to give them licence some times to walk, three or four together, the juniors with the seniors (refraining the town) about the hills and fields to recreate their minds and to lax their veins, whereby they may be more apt to continue both day and night in the service of God. Yet we most heartily desire you to suffer us to have some poor honest woman to keep us if any pestifer(ous) plague or distress of sickness do fall amongst us, as it hath been there of long consuetude . . . [15]

No reply appears to have been received to this letter.

Having received copious evidence from his commissioners of wrong-doing, laxity and scandal in many monastic houses throughout the country, Cromwell was able to persuade Parliament early in 1536 to pass an Act for the Dissolution of the Lesser Monasteries, whereby all religious houses with a net annual income of less than £200 were to be suppressed and all their lands, estates and property given to the King. Three of the Bristol houses came within the terms of this Act, but St James Priory was exempted because it was a subsidiary house of Tewkesbury abbey, and St Mark's escaped because it was regarded as a hospital rather than a monastery, even though it had been visited by Layton in 1535. This left only St Mary Magdalen, the poor house of nuns at the foot of St Michael's Hill where there were only two inmates.

---

15. Public Record Office SP1/96/32–3, quoted in J. Youings, *The Dissolution of the Monasteries*, 1971, 153.

This was suppressed and its endowments were seized by the Crown. In order to deal with all the property coming to the Crown from the suppressed monastic houses, a new government department was set up, the Court of Augmentations, and the new Court appointed commissioners in each county to survey the properties, ensure the departure of the inmates and to administer the property on behalf of the Crown. In Bristol the local commissioners were Thomas White and Nicholas Thorne. They assessed the net income of the nunnery of St Mary Magdalen as £21 13s 2d *per annum* and reported that there were two nuns, 'by report of honest conversation, whereof one professed being impotent and aged, the other a young novice desiring continuance in religion'. The elderly nun was Eleanor Graunte who had been appointed prioress in 1521.[16] There was also a man servant and a woman laundress. The house was obviously very poor, the lead and bells were found to be worth only 19s 0d, the 'stuff of the household' was valued at a mere 14s 0d, and the ornaments and treasure in the chapel were assessed at only £3 2s 10d, although the house itself was said to be 'in convenient reparation' and the nunnery was not in debt.[17] Unlike later suppressions, no pensions were awarded to the religious at this time and there is no evidence of what happened to the two nuns. In March 1537 the nunnery and its grounds were leased by the Crown to Dame Joan Guildeford, widow, for 21 years at an annual rent of 13s 4d and it was turned into a private dwelling. When John Leland saw the building early in the 1540s it was well-established as a dwelling and he described it as 'a howse of nunnes suppressyd . . . Master Wiks dwellythe in this howse'.[18]

Following the closure of the smaller monasteries in 1536, heavy pressure was then put upon the larger religious houses by Cromwell and his commissioners to persuade them to surrender voluntarily, offering generous pensions to those who would do so. During the early months of 1538 a few of the west-country monasteries, including Muchelney, Kingswood and Llanthony-by-Glouester, succumbed and surrendered all their property and possessions into the King's hands. In Bristol, however, the houses

16. *L. & P. Henry VIII*, XI, 307.
17. P.R.O. SC12/33/37.
18. Gloucester Public Library, Hockaday Abstracts, 436; L. Toulmin Smith, *Leland's Itinerary*, 1910, V, 88–9.

of St Augustine's, St James and St Mark's refused to give up and the ancient round of conventual services and monastic life continued. But during the summer of 1538 Bristol was greatly affected by the suppression of the four friaries. Unlike the monasteries, the friaries possessed little wealth, for the friars were dedicated to poverty. In the final years of their existence and through all the religious changes, many friars had become discouraged and demoralised; some had fled abroad, charitable donations from the laity had diminished and many of the friaries were in debt. Their closure brought little wealth to the Crown, but many friars were conservative in their religious views and they were powerful and experienced preachers, so that Cromwell evidently felt that they should be disbanded. The task of persuading the friars all over the country to give up their way of life and 'voluntarily' surrender their houses was entrusted to Richard Ingworth, who had himself been a Dominican friar and had become head of the English Dominicans. In February 1538 he had been made suffragan bishop of Dover. Ingworth travelled across England during May and June 1538, receiving the surrender of friaries in the towns along his way. At Gloucester he supervised the closure of the three friaries in the town and then travelled on to Marlborough and Winchester, eventually arriving at Bristol in July 1538.

The Bishop found the four friaries in Bristol poverty-stricken and badly in debt, while the friars were obviously demoralised and uncertain, anxious about their future. He reported to Cromwell that 'The substance in the more part of the houses is very small; in divers places little more than the debts; and the clamour of poor men to whom money is owing is too tedious'.[19] With the Carmelites or White Friars in Bristol Bishop Ingworth had little difficulty, for the house was severely in debt and the four friars were quite willing to surrender everything to the Crown. The Prior had fled taking most of the valuables of the house with him and the remaining friars saw no alternative but to abandon their way of life. On 28 July 1538 Ingworth arranged for them to be brought before the Mayor, where all signed the formal statement declaring that

> they voluntarily did leave their house in Bristol because they perceived that they before had divers priors the which had sold and

---

19. *L. & P. Henry*, XIII(i), 391.

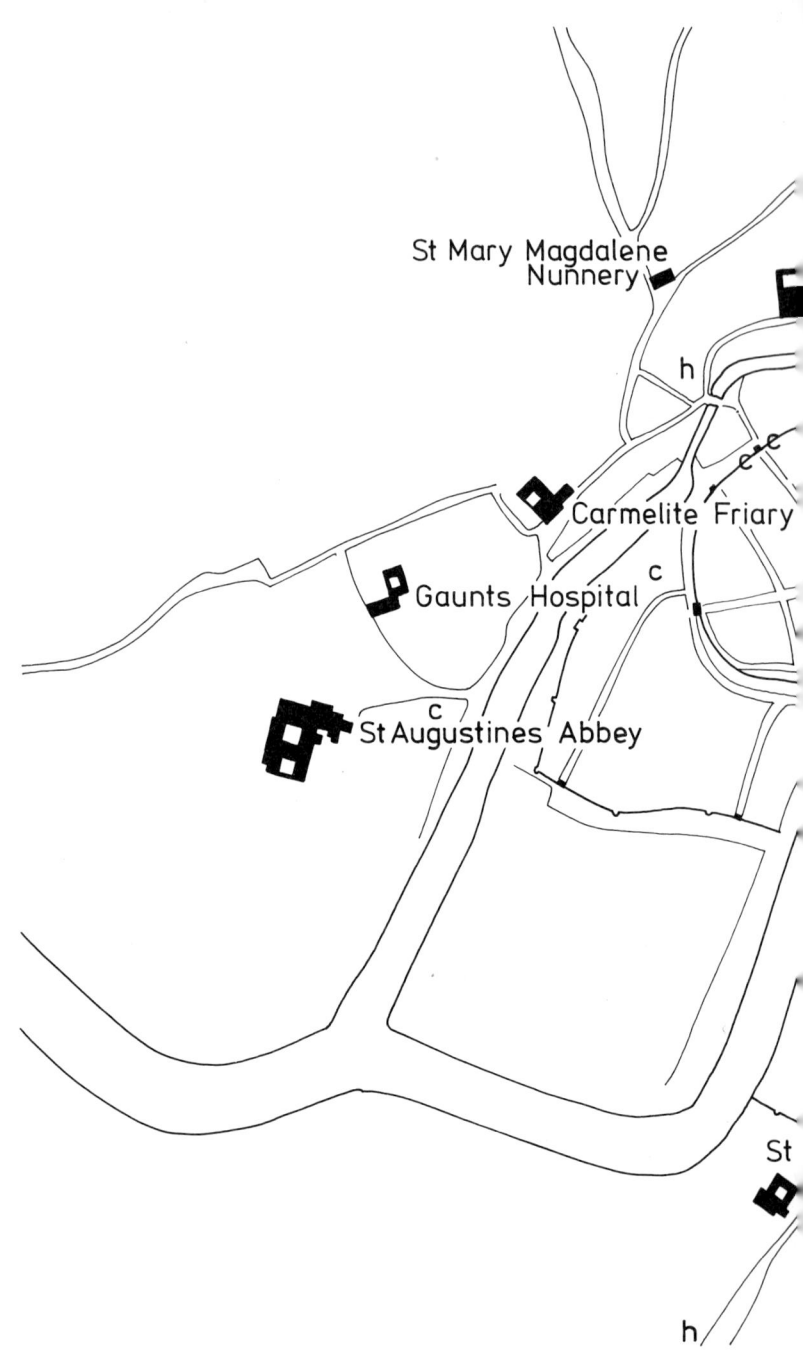

The Religious Houses of Medieval Bristol
(M. Aston)

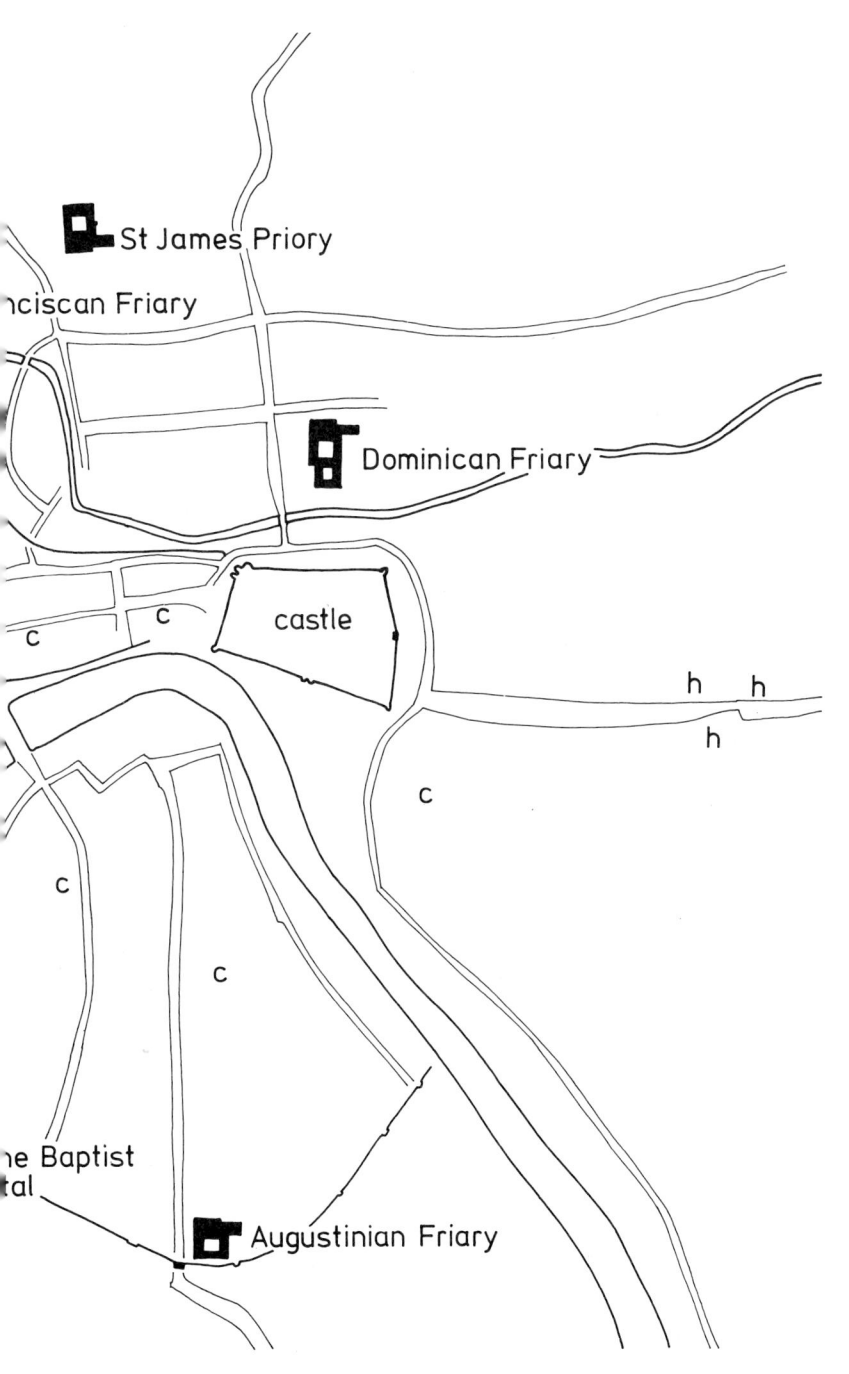

plundered all the jewels and substance with other ornaments and stuff of the house, and yet left them in debt and no things to live with, and considering that the charity of the people is very small so that they cannot see how to continue and live in their house, wherefore voluntarily they give their house into the visitor's hands to the King's use . . .

>Thomas Clifton, sub-prior
>Thomas Wraxall
>Simon Wagon *als* Vagan
>John Hooper[20]

The Carmelite friary stood near the site of the present Colston Hall and was close to the town overlooking the busy harbour in the river Frome, while the garden stretched up the hillside as far as the present Red Lodge. In spite of its poverty, Bishop Ingworth was obviously impressed by the excellence of the building and its attractive site, as well as by the water supply for the friary which still runs in a conduit from Brandon Hill and down Park Street, and an off-shoot crosses the Frome and continues to flow out of the cock by St John's church on the city wall. The Bishop wrote to Cromwell that

> It is a goodly house in building, meet for a great man, no rents but their gardens. There is a chapel and an aisle of the church, and divers gutters, spouts and conduits of lead, the rest all tile and slate. A goodly laver and conduit coming to it. The house was in debt above £16, of the which paid £8, the rest discharged by pledges.[21]

As will be shown later, the site and buildings of the Carmelites were purchased by the Corporation of Bristol soon after the suppression; later in the sixteenth centuy they were acquired by John Young, a wealthy gentleman with estates in Dorset and Wiltshire. He built the 'Great House' on the site where he entertained Queen Elizabeth with lavish hospitality in 1574 and was knighted by the Queen. The Red Lodge was built at the end of the former garden of the friary in 1590.

The other three Bristol friaries did not surrender quite so readily or easily; Bishop Ingworth reported that they were 'stiff' in their opposition in spite of their poverty and difficulties, and he was

---

20. G.E. Weare, *Collectanea*, 1893, 75.
21. *Ibid*.

forced to leave them until the autumn of 1538, while he went to urge and supervise the closure of friaries elsewhere. He returned to Bristol early in September 1538 to put further pressure on the friars to make 'voluntary' surrenders of their houses. The first to give way was the Augustinian friary at Temple Gate. The prior, Nicholas Sandford, was reluctant to relinquish his office on the grounds that he had been appointed for life, but the poverty of his friary was such that he had been forced to sell much of the plate and had even resorted to selling the trees that stood around the friary. On 10 September 1538 therefore the Augustinian friars signed a final declaration:

> Memorandum, We the prior and convente of the Austin friars of Bristow without any manner of coercion or counsel do give our house into the hands of the lorde visitor to the King's use, desiring his grace to be good and gracious to us.

This was signed by the prior and seven friars. The inventory of the friary lists the church, vestry, hall and kitchen. There were few possessions of any value, and the lead had to be stripped from the friary roof to meet their debts. In 1544 the buildings were conveyed by the Crown to a royal official, Maurice Dennys.[22]

On the same day, 10 September 1538, Bishop Ingworth received the surrender of the Franciscans or Grey Friars in Lewins Mead. Their prior, Robert Sanderson, had already left and the six friars were without leadership and heavily in debt, and the inventory of their possessions reveals the poverty and basic nature of their existence. Bishop Ingworth took away a cross from the church 'doubting whether it be silver or no' and a chalice, the both articles together weighing fifty-one ounces. There were also various vestments in the church, a table and trestles in the hall, a few poor forms, cupboards and two chairs in the parlour and buttery. In the chambers were 'ii bedsteds, iii chests and a cheyer', while there were various pots and pans in the kitchen. The furniture and possessions hardly seem sufficient to have met the needs of six friars. The Bishop noted that 'there be many debtors that call for debts divers . . . but none be paide, the cause is the warden is not here to know whether the debts be all owing or no'. In March 1539

---

22. *Ibid.*, 80–3, 102; Gloucester Public Library, Hockaday Abstracts, 436.

the site and buildings were leased by the Crown to a Bristol merchant, William Chester.[23]

Finally, Bishop Ingworth received the surrender of the Dominican friars in Broadmead. The friary of the Dominicans or Black Friars was more extensive and apparently less poverty-stricken than the three other Bristol friaries. It had a very large church which like the other friary churches was designed for preaching and to hold a large congregation. It was in the Black Friars' church that Hugh Latimer preached one of his controversial Lenten semons in 1533. To the south of the church was the Great Cloister and around it the 'dorter' or dormitory and the 'frater' or dining hall. There was also a chapter house, infirmary and other buildings, while the site also included a large orchard. The whole site was seven acres in extent. In the friars' church the Guild of Bakers had a chapel and maintained a light there before the altar of their patron, St Clement, while the Mayor and Corporation of Bristol heard an annual sermon in the church on the second Sunday in Advent. On 10 September 1538 the prior, Thomas Parker, and his four friars finally abandoned their way of life and declared that they yielded up their friary to the King 'with one assent and consent'.[24]

From the Dominican friary church Bishop Ingworth removed 176 ounces of plate, including two chalices, a censer, a broken cross set with stones, a pyx or receptacle for the Blessed Sacrament and two candlesticks. He also sold vestments for £6 16s 8d to pay the debts of the friary, the remaining goods were delivered to the local commissioners, Robert Woodwarde and John Amerycke for safekeeping. The domestic furniture included three feather beds, three chairs, two tables, three carpets and two cupboards. In the kitchen were 'iv gret brasse potts and ii lytyll potts with a possenet' together with sundry kettles, plates and dishes. Curiously, the friars also possessed 'iii pewter pots to put flowers in', but presumably these were for use in the church.

The site and buildings were sold by the Crown in 1539 for £37 10s 0d to William Chester, who had also acquired the Franciscan friary. Chester was a wealthy merchant and prominent citizen; he was sheriff of Bristol in 1522, mayor in 1537 and 1552 and M.P. for the city in 1555. He lived in a large house in

---

23. P.R.O. E117/14/35; *L. & P. Henry VIII*, XV, 831 (67).
24. G.E. Weare, *op. cit.*, 83–4.

Broadmead to which he added the lands of the Black friars. Alone of the Bristol friaries, parts of the Dominicans' house survive, since it later became a Quaker meeting house and is now known by the title of Quaker Friars.[25]

The friars themselves received 'capacities' or licences to become secular priests and most seem to have left Bristol. Unlike the monks, they received no pensions from the state and whereas the monks often entered the monastery at an early age and had relatives and connections in the local area, the friars frequently had no such ties and nothing to keep them in Bristol. The subsequent careers of a few friars are known. For example, Ralph Darle, a Bristol Dominican, became vicar of North Curry in Somerset; Thomas Lewis and Thomas Lee, Bristol Franciscans, also obtained benefices in Somerset. Most is known about the Augustinian canons, three of whom became chantry priests in Bristol.[26] Rather more detail survives about the prior of the Augustinians, Nicholas Sandford, since in a dispute of 1543 over a will to which he had been a witness, he stated that he had been born at Thorpe Salvyn in Yorkshire, that he was prior of the Austin friars for four years and that after the suppression he had become vicar of Bedminster.[27] The rest of the friars vanished without trace from the Bristol scene; and the four friaries which had for three centuries been so prominent in Bristol life and whose friars had been such popular preachers and workers among the poor, disappeared completely, apparently without any voice raised in their defence or any opposition to their suppression.

By the autumn of 1538 the three houses, St Augustine's, St Mark's and St James, remained still untouched; and for a further year nothing happened, although throughout the country religious houses were being surrendered one after the other, so that by the final months of 1539 only a few survived. In December 1539 the royal commissioners made their final onslaught on Bristol. On 9 December 1539 St Mark's or the Gaunts Hospital was suppressed. Its annual income was assessed at £165 2s 4d. The master, John

---

25. *Ibid.*, 84–7; Gloucester Public Library, Hockaday Abstracts, 436.
26. G. Baskerville, 'The Dispossessed Religious of Gloucestershire', *Bristol & Gloucestershire Archaeological Society Transactions*, 49, 1927, 63–122.
27. F.W. Weaver, ed., 'Somerset Medieval Wills 1531–58', *Somerset Record Society*, 21, 1905, 44–6.

Colman, received a pension of £40 *per annum*; other pensions were awarded as follows: 'Richard Fechet, priest, £6 13s 4d *per annum*; John Eles, priest to be curate of the parish church of St Mark with £8 0s 0d *per annum* over and above the small tithes and oblations; if he refuse the said cure to have but £6 0s 0d *per annum*; Thos. Pinchyn, clerk, £6 0s 0d *per annum*'. In addition £10 9s 4d was paid to sixteen men, children, choristers and servants who were resident in the hospital, and they were evicted.

In May 1541 the site and much of the property of St Mark's was purchased from the Crown by the mayor and commonalty of Bristol for £1,000 and an annual rent of £20. The purchase included lands in Bristol, Gloucestershire and Somerset and included the manor of Hampe in Somerset which had belonged to Athelney abbey, and other lands and property which had belonged to the nunnery of St Mary Magdalen, to the Grey Friars and the White Friars in Bristol, together with sundry other parcels of land.[28] This was a remarkable and far-sighted purchase by the ruling body of Bristol and ensured that the city was well-endowed with a large annual income from its widespread lands. It also meant that St Mark's church came into the possession of the Corporation of Bristol, becoming the Lord Mayor's chapel. On the same day that St Mark's Hospital was suppressed, St Augustine's abbey, which was by far the richest and most splendid of all the religious houses of Bristol, also surrendered to the Crown. It seems likely that almost until the very end the abbot, William Burton, hoped somehow to avoid closure, or possibly wished to ingratiate himself with Cromwell merely to ensure better treatment for himself and his canons. Whatever his motives, he wrote to Cromwell on 21 February 1539 an obsequious letter thanking him for his great goodness to the monastery and sending him a gift of 20 nobles (£6 13s 4d). The position of St Augustine's was made even more difficult in July 1539 by the death of William Burton, who had been abbot since 1525. Although monasteries were being closed throughout the country, nonetheless a successor was elected and Morgan Gwilliam, who had been the prior, became abbot on 24 August 1539, so he had been in office for only a few weeks when the end came.[29] When Morgan Gwilliam and his

---

28. *L. & P. Henry VIII*, XIV(i) 661; XV, 139; XVI, 878(10). *V.C.H. Gloucestershire*, II, 1907, 117; *Bristol & Gloucestershire Archaeological Society Transactions*, LV, 1933, 151–90.
29. *L. & P. Henry VIII*, XIV(i), 33, 1354(39); XIV(ii) 113(27).

Gatehouse to St Augustine's Abbey

The lower part of this impressive entrance dates from the twelfth century, while the upper stages were rebuilt by Abbot John Newland or Nailheart (1481–1515), and was much restored in the nineteenth century

11 canons surrendered the house to the royal commissioners on 9 December 1539 its clear yearly value was assessed at £692 2s 7d, besides £70 3s 4d 'in fees and annuities granted to divers persons for term of life'. Like the heads of most religious houses, the recently-appointed abbot, Morgan Gwilliam was awarded a very generous pension. He received £80 0s 0d *per annum*, the manor house which had formerly belonged to the abbey at Abbots Leigh, together with the orchard, garden and dovecote there, and twenty cartloads of wood and underwood for fuel each year from the woods of the manor of Abbots Leigh.[30] The canons got much smaller but nonetheless adequate pensions, ranging from £8 0s 0d to £6 0s 0d *per annum*, according to their seniority within the monastery. In addition, each of the canons received a gift of £2 0s 0d from the Crown as an additional inducement to make a voluntary surrender of their house.[31]

In addition to the religious, there were also forty-six officers of the household and servants employed in the abbey, all of whom were paid their wages and dismissed by the royal commissioners. Although not among the top rank of west-country religious houses in terms of wealth, St Augustine's was very well endowed and its possessions, treasures and furnishings were very fine and valuable. The lead covering the roofs of the monastic church and buildings was especially valuable and the royal commissioners estimated that there were 130 fodders or fothers of lead (a fother was $19\frac{1}{2}$ cwt, so there were more than 126 tons of lead on the building). In addition, they listed ten bells in the tower and the following precious objects:

> Jewels reserved to the use of the King's Majesty:
> Mitres garnished with silver gilt ragged pearls and counterfeit stones.
> Certain garnishing of vestments of silver gilt duameld and set with small pearls
> Plate of silver reserved to the use of the King's Majesty:
>
> | Silver gilt | 229 ounces | |
> |---|---|---|
> | Silver parcel gilt | 151 ounces | 526 ounces |
> | Silver white | 146 ounces | |
>
> Ornaments, goods and chattells sold by the Commissioners £103 13s 7d.

---

30. Gloucester Public Library, Hockaday Abstracts, 428.
31. *L. & P. Henry VIII*, XIV(ii) 660.

The commissioners also paid off various outstanding debts for victuals, cloth, wax, salt, wine and spices which amounted in total to £58 10s 2d.

On 14 March 1541 the abbey and its precinct including houses, orchards, gardens, ponds, two marshes of about thirty-two acres, a pasture called Cantock's Close and other former abbey lands were leased to William Greensmith, yeoman, of Hampton, Middlesex. A year later the lease was revoked when the former abbey church became the cathedral of the newly-created diocese of Bristol and the former abbot's lodging became the bishop's palace.[32] The annual income provided for the bishop, dean and six canons of the new cathedral totalled £697 3s 11d and very closely matched the annual income of the former abbey.

Finally, on 9 January 1540 the ancient and wealthy Benedictine abbey of Tewkesbury was surrendered by the abbot and thirty-eight monks, and with Tewkesbury was suppressed the priory of St James, its cell in Bristol, although the priory may have been already abandoned by the monks before the final end at Tewkesbury. The prior of St James, Robert Cicestre, received a pension of £13 6s 8d *per annum* and the two monks were also granted pensions by the Crown. It may be that the monks of St James priory had anticipated the closure of their house, since they had already leased much of the property to Anthony Kingston, a royal official and courtier, whose family was to profit handsomely from the dispersal of monastic lands. After the final suppression Kingston was granted a lease of the lands and property of St James Priory by the Crown.[33] Because of an agreement which had been made in 1374 between the Priory and the townspeople living nearby, the nave of the Priory church had become parochial and was used for parish worship while the choir was reserved for the monks. At the suppression therefore, the nave, with its remarkable Romanesque west front, was regarded as a parish church and was allowed to remain, but the chancel was demolished.

Glastonbury, the richest and most ancient of all the west-country monasteries, had been forcibly suppressed during the autumn of 1539 and the elderly abbot, Richard Whiting, and two of his monks had been executed on Glastonbury Tor on 15 November 1539 for refusing to surrender the goods and treasures

---

32. Gloucester Public Library, Hockaday Abstracts, 428.
33. *Ibid.*, 438.

of their monastery. The last of the west-country monasteries were dissolved soon afterwards, St Augustine's, Bristol on 9 December, Malmesbury on 15 December, Cirencester 19 December, Hailes 24 December 1539. St Peter's abbey at Gloucester was dissolved on 2 January 1540, and Tewkesbury, the last of the west-country monasteries together with its cell of St James in Bristol, surrendered on 9 January 1540. Thus monasticism came to an end and all the property passed to the Crown, without any protest or any west-country voices raised in support of the monks and nuns.[34] No evidence survives as to the feelings of the Bristol monks when their ancient institutions were closed for ever. We do not know with what attitude of eagerness or reluctance they signed their assent to the Royal Supremacy in 1534, nor with what feelings of release or regret they finally agreed to succumb to the pressure from the royal commissioners or to the inducement of generous pensions and gifts and surrender their houses in 1539. Certainly the friars appear to have been reluctant to go, in spite of their poverty and the problems they faced, but none of the Bristol religious left the sort of anguished letter written by Edmund Horde, the last prior of the Carthusian house at Hinton Charterhouse, south of Bath, who in a bitter struggle with his conscience wondered how he could give up the monastery

> which is not ours to give, but dedicate to Almighty God for service to be done to his honour continually. . . .

Only Richard Whiting, the abbot of Glastonbury, and two of his monks remained steadfast to the death and were executed for their refusal to surrender. In spite of his misgivings, Edmund Horde eventually surrendered his house to the Crown, as did the monks and canons of Bristol, but sadly we have no indication of their feelings when they left their monasteries and their regular, ordered way of life for the last time.

The subsequent careers of many of the monks, friars and canons who were evicted from the religious houses of Bristol remain uncertain and apart from lists of pensions we have no knowledge of what happened to them. For a few, however, their fortunes can

---

34. J.H. Bettey, *Suppression of the Monasteries in the West Country*, 1989.

Chapel of St Mark's or the Gaunts Hospital

The fourteenth-century street frontage of the remarkably ornate chapel which was acquired by the mayor and corporation of Bristol and became the Lord Mayor's Chapel

be traced in some detail.[35] By far the highest pension was awarded to Morgan Gwilliam, the abbot of St Augustine's, who received £80 *per annum* as well as the manor house of Abbots Leigh and other perquisites. He appears not to have remained at Abbots Leigh, but to have gone to the Isle of Wight, where he died in 1544. Some of the canons of St Augustine's had evidently anticipated the end of their abbey and had secured grants or promises of parish livings, curacies or chantry foundations for themselves. Thus when in 1542, Nicholas Corbett was instituted as vicar of Pawlett, Somerset, one of the parishes which had been in the patronage of St Augustine's abbey, his institution was said to be 'by reason of a grant of the late abbot'. Several other canons also obtained parish benefices. The prior, Humphrey Heymond, became vicar of All Saints', Bristol, another former abbey parish; Henry Parye became curate of Horfield, William Wrington became a chantry priest at Berkeley and Richard Oriell became a chantry priest and later vicar of Bedminster. Many of these men had local ties and remained in the region. Apart from the abbot and one of the canons, Richard Carsy, who accompanied him to the Isle of Wight, only one other, Richard Hughes, moved farther afield, becoming rector of Brandeston in Norfolk.

The later careers of some of the friars have already been described, but since they were not awarded pensions they are more difficult to trace. It is also difficult to track the movements of the monks of St James priory since their names are included without distinction in the list of thirty-eight monks who belonged to Tewkesbury abbey when it was suppressed. One of the chaplains of St Mark's, John Ellis, remained there as parish priest following the suppression of the hospital.

After all the religious changes of the later years of Henry VIII and the reign of Edward VI, a list of pensions still being paid to the former inmates of religious houses was compiled during the reign of Queen Mary in 1555. This shows that Robert Cicestre, the former prior of St James, was still receiving his pension of £13 6s 8d *per annum* and that five former canons of St Augustine's were still alive and collecting pensions. They were John Rastle,

---

35. Much of the following section is based on G. Baskerville, 'The Dispossessed Religious of Gloucestershire', *Bristol & Gloucestershire Archaeological Society Transactions*, 49, 1927, 63–122.

Richard Oriell, Richard Carsey, Richard Hughes and William Underwood.

As we have seen, the church of the Augustinian canons survived because it became the cathedral of the new diocese of Bristol in 1542, while many of its buildings were preserved for the bishop and canons of the cathedral. Likewise, St Mark's church was regarded as parochial and survived, as did the nave of St James priory, but at both places the domestic buildings seem to have been demolished rapidly. The monks' choir and conventual buildings of St James were destroyed by the new owners, Henry Brayne and William Kingston. When John Leland visited the site early in the 1540s he described the former priory as a ruin, 'It standeth by Brode meade by northe from the Castle on a hilly ground, and the ruins of it standeth hard buttynge to the easte ende of the paroche churche. This St James was a cell to Tewkesberye'.[36] Likewise, the large churches of the friaries were quickly destroyed. The new owners, who had bought these buildings from the Crown, sought to recoup their outlay by selling the cut stone and tiles for building work, so that the once-splendid buildings very quickly became ruins. In the Ledger of the wealthy Bristol merchant, John Smythe, he records payments in 1543 for 'stones from the Fryers' as well as money laid out in rent for 'my garden at the White Fryers'. The churchwardens' accounts of the numerous Bristol churches also show that they used the former religious houses as convenient sources of building materials, especially during the reign of Queen Mary, when they were required to replace in their churches so many of the furnishings which had been discarded or destroyed during the previous reign. Thus in 1553–4 the churchwardens of St Werburgh's paid for stone to be brought from the derelict house of Black Friars in Broad Mead in order to re-build the stone altars and the Easter Sepulchre, which had been torn out only a few years before. Similarly, the Corporation of Bristol applied to Cromwell for stone and timber from the friaries in order to repair tenements and construct a new wharf.[37]

---

36. L. Toulmin Smith, ed., *Leland's Itinerary*, 1910. V, 88.
37. J. Vanes, ed., 'The Ledger of John Smythe 1538–1550', *Bristol Record Society*, XXVIII, 1975, 229; J.H. Bettey, *Bristol Parish Churches during the Reformation*, Bristol Historical Association, 1979, 14; *L. & P. Henry VIII*, XIII, 322.

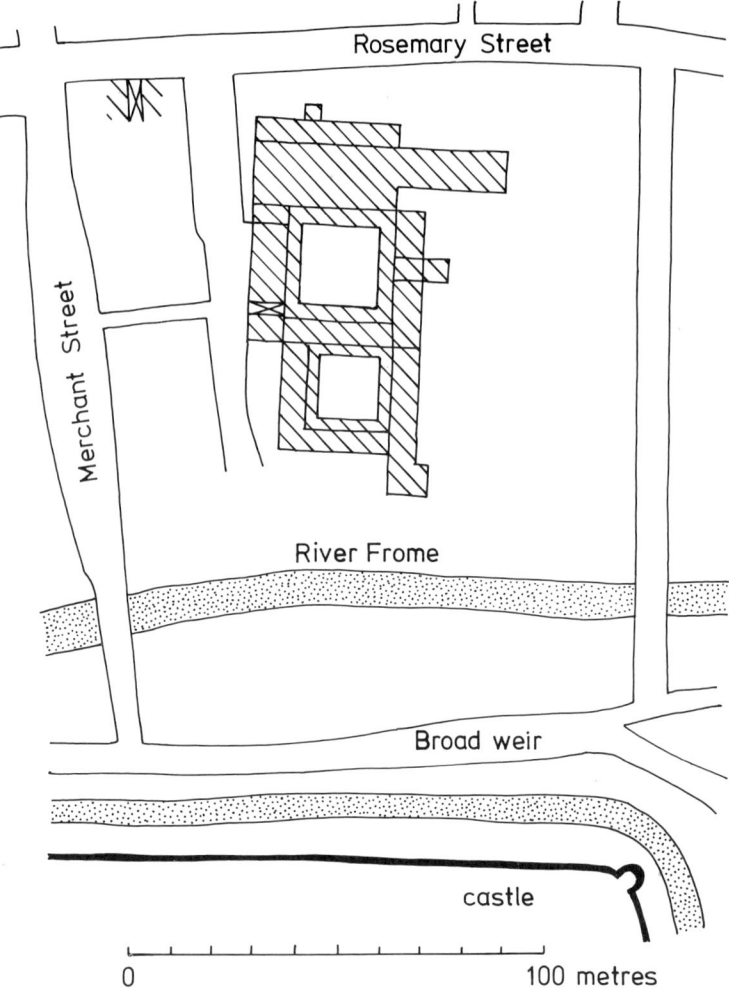

The Plan of the Dominican Friary in Broadmead

The extensive site was on the bank of the river Frome, and the plan shows the church, the great cloister which was surrounded by the sacristy, chapter house, frater and dorter, and the lesser cloister which included the infirmary. The plan also shows the gatehouse at the junction of Merchant Street and Rosemary Street
(Reconstruction by M. Aston)

Most of the former monastic lands and buildings were acquired by two classes in the community, either by royal servants, officials and courtiers or by local gentry and merchants. Thus royal officials such as Henry Brayne, William Popley, the Berkeleys, the Kingston family of Painswick or the royal physician and Bristolian, George Owen, were all in a good position to obtain former monastic land, and made the most of the opportunity. Likewise, local gentry such as the Poyntz family of Iron Acton or the Bayntons and Pophams or merchants such as John Smythe, John Cutte, William Chester and Thomas White were able to find the necessary money to buy former monastic land, both for themselves and also for the Corporation of Bristol. Of the purchases by the Mayor and commonalty of Bristol, by far the most notable was made on 6 May 1541, when lands which had belonged to St Mark's Hospital, the Grey Friars and the White Friars, together with other former monastic land, were purchased for £1,000 with far-reaching effects upon the later wealth of the city of Bristol.[38]

During the decade after the dissolution, the lands and buildings of the Bristol religious houses, like those throughout the whole country, were sold and re-sold and passed into the hands of numerous different people, so that by 1553, when Queen Mary came to the throne determined fully to restore Catholicism, she was unable to breathe fresh life into the monasteries. By then the lands were dispersed, the churches demolished and the buildings either destroyed or converted to other uses; as a consequence there were many influential people with a vested interest in ensuring that the monasteries were not revived. Meanwhile a generation was growing up who had never known the monasteries and for whom the once-familiar figures of monks and nuns, canons and friars had never been the normal background to their daily lives. With the accession of Elizabeth in 1558 and the abandoning of Catholicism, all hope of a return of monasticism or of the revival of the religious houses vanished.

---

38. R.C. Latham, ed., 'Bristol Charters 1509–1899, *Bristol Record Society*, XII, 1946, 84–92.

ACKNOWLEDGEMENTS AND NOTE ON SOURCES

I am grateful to Professor McGrath for his helpful comments and criticisms and to my colleague Michael Aston who has discussed the subject with me on many occasions and who kindly drew the map of the Bristol religious houses and the plan of the Dominican friary. I am also indebted to Nicholas Lee of the University Library for his help in finding illustrations from the Library collection.

The main sources which have been consulted are listed in the footnotes. The best and most comprehensive account of the dissolution on a national scale is given by David Knowles, *The Religious Orders in England*, III, CUP, 2nd edition, 1971. The major documentary sources are discussed with numerous examples in Joyce Youings, *The Dissolution of the Monasteries*, Allen & Unwin, 1971; the full story of the dissolution throughout the Bristol region and an account of the manifold effects which this produced is told in J.H. Bettey, *The Suppression of the Monasteries in the West Country*, Alan Sutton, 1989.